Origami Book for Beginners

A Step-by-Step Introduction to the Japanese Art of Paper Folding for Kids & Adults

Yuto Kanazawa

Table of Contents

Introduction

Origami is an ancient art form with a history as old and rich as the paper it is made of. As paper evolved and became more refined, so did the art of origami, and as the art grew, it became more popular and spread across the entire world. While cultures all over the world have their own forms of paper folding art, the Japanese art of origami is the art form that has become the most popular and taken the world by storm.

Origami can be as simple or complex as the artist wishes. Designs like a plain, simple heart or dog can be a great introduction to the art for children who, as they progress, may move on to something that takes a little more skill like a paper crane or rhinoceros. Dedicated artists can learn to form gorgeous masterpieces, like an intricate Chinese dragon with individual scales, all folded from a single piece of paper. This is a great art to learn, as the ease with which you can get started is great for beginners. Not to mention that it is one of the most affordable art forms available since even if you can't get your hands on proper origami paper, you can still get a lot of practice done with any paper you've got laying around the house or office.

Origami is a wonderful art form, and understanding a little more about where it comes from can help you appreciate it on a deeper level.

What is Origami?

In truth, the name says it all. The word origami is built up of two Japanese words: *'oru'*, which translates to *'to fold'*, and *'kami'*, which translates to *'paper'*. As such, origami is the art of folding animals, flowers, figures, boxes, trees, etc. out of paper. An important element of origami is that the paper isn't cut or torn in any way. The paper also can't be glued or taped down to hold any edges or corners in place. Instead, clever folds and tucks are used to do that.

Traditionally, each origami figure is folded using a single piece of paper, but more modern designs have incorporated ways to fold two or three pieces together for a larger project. It is also traditional not to make any marks on the origami with a pen or pencil, either to mark fold lines or as decoration. True origami paper also has one blank side and one colored side, but you can still use any paper you like as long as it suits your needs.

A Quick History of Origami

The exact origin of paper folding as an art form, in general, is not certain, and many believe the origins to be older than paper itself when decorative folding techniques were applied to other pliable materials like silk and leather. When paper was first created in China in 105 AD, it was discovered to be the perfect material for folding: more loose and flexible than leather, and thus capable of much finer detail, but sturdier than silk and capable of holding its shape much better. Somewhere between the sixth and seventh century, this art was brought to Japan and the seeds of origami were sown. Known as *origata* at the time, the art of paper folding was an exclusive ritual performed by the samurai and holy men and women, due to the rarity of paper. As an element of Shintō rituals, decorative boxes and envelopes were folded out of paper and used to wrap offerings given to the gods. It also became popular to use origata to present betrothal and wedding gifts.

In the Edo period, from 1603 to 1868, handmade *washi* paper became more readily available and allowed paper folding to become a popular hobby among the commoners, for both adults and children. This more 'common' and less ritualistic form of paper folding became known as origami. Other than just a fun way to pass the time, commoners used origami as a cheap, easy way to decorate their homes and gifts. As with most elements of Japanese art, it was most common to fold origami figures that resemble elements of nature, such as animals, plants, and even floral patterns. Origami became so popular during this time period that it was incorporated into other forms of art, and there were even entire paintings depicting women folding origami in their homes.

Initially, the figures folded were fairly simple and easy, but as the art was practiced, more techniques and more intricate designs were discovered and shared. During this time, the art developed into a tradition and a part of the culture with a deeper meaning. The cultural significance associated with certain animals and other symbols and figures were transferred to their origami counterparts, and even different types of folds were given some significance. In 1797, a book called *Hiden Senbazuru Origata*, or *The Secret of Folding 1000 Paper Cranes*, was published by Akisato Rito, in which he explains the cultural significance of the art and introduces 49 different ways of folding paper cranes. This was the first-ever written record of the art.

In 1954, the traditional art of origami was revolutionized when Akira Yoshizawa published a book called *Atarashi Origami Geijutsu*, which translates to *The New Origami Art*. In this book, the author not only introduced the concept of using origami as an educational tool to help teach children certain basic math concepts, but he also used new patterns that encouraged origami artists to cut, tear, wet, and glue the paper to make intricate new figures. With these new origami designs, the artists were no longer restricted to using only one square piece of paper, and the art form enjoyed a new surge in popularity. This book also helped spread the art form to the rest of the world and turn the Japanese art of paper folding into a worldwide sensation.

Paper Folding in Europe

On the other side of the world, another form of paper folding was being born. There are believed to be two main origins of this art in Europe, the first being a series of geometric, mathematical forms of folding. These specific patterns were introduced to Spain by the Moors. The Spanish took to this new concept very well and turned it into their own, unique art form called *pajarita*.

Another European paper folding origin carries more similarities with Japanese origami, as it was also developed from a different form of folding art. In the early seventeenth century, it was extremely popular to fold napkins into intricate geometric patterns and three-dimensional figures. This was especially popular among the noble-born or wealthy, who used these napkin folding techniques to impress guests during celebrations or dinner parties. During this time, it wasn't unusual to apply some of these folding techniques to paper among the wealthier families, but this was considered a fun hobby or pastime rather than a true craft or art form.

It was only in the nineteenth century that paper folding became popular after a man called Friedrich Fröbel brought the concept into kindergartens. One of the recreational and educational activities in the curriculum was paper folding, in which napkin folding techniques were applied to help children fold cute, fun figures. When the children showed their parents what they'd learned, it sparked an interest in the adult population. As this new twist on napkin folding became increasingly popular and spread throughout Europe, new techniques were applied, and paper folding evolved into its own art form. As European and Japanese cultures met and began to interact with each other, napkin and paper folding techniques were shared and the art became even more interesting and diverse.

Modern Origami

The modern origami we know today has some significant differences from the art form practiced during the Edo period.

First and foremost is the fact that credit is given to those who create new origami folding sequences. Traditionally, origami techniques and sequences were spread orally from generation to generation, such as a woman teaching an origami sequence to her children and their friends which she had learned from her own mother. When new folding sequences were created, they were introduced to the community anonymously. As an example, a young woman creates a new sequence and shows it to her friends. All these friends then show this new sequence to their friends, and so on until the entire village has learned the new sequence and no one can quite remember where it started. As a result, the brilliant creators of these techniques and sequences were left unknown to history, and no one can trace a sequence to its point of origin.

This changed in the twentieth century when a Sōtō priest became the first man to ever register and patent an origami sequence, claiming credit for his new creation. This monumental act inspired a new belief that those with the intellect and artistry to create new sequences should receive due credit for their skills. This meant that more and more artists began patenting their work and new origami sequences were even copyrighted. This made origami a much more personal form of art. Along with the limited nature of teaching a sequence orally, this format also created a problem with accessibility. If you wanted to learn a specific origami sequence, you had to find someone who knew how to fold it and then convince them to teach it to you. Because of this, sequences usually stayed within the families or communities where they were created, and even though there were some who wrote down instructions for their sequences, everyone had their own way of doing it, and language remained a barrier.

In the 1930s, a man called Akira Yoshizawa devised a system of documenting folding sequences through the use of diagrams, lines, and arrows. This diagram system was easy to understand and did not have the limitations that language barriers imposed, and twenty years later, origami folding sequences began to be published worldwide using this system. This new availability and easy access to sequences made a large contribution to the new surge of popularity the art of origami has experienced in modern society.

Another significant difference between traditional and modern origami is the freedom in application and use of origami. With the publication of *The New Origami Art* and the new techniques introduced through different cultures, origami artists were allowed much more freedom, being able to modify their paper to better suit their designs, and a whole wave of new origami creations was let out into the world, both for those practicing origami as a hobby and those pursuing the art in professional circles. Artists were allowed to create much more intricate and sturdy designs and folding sequences. Even those who follow the traditional methods of using a single piece of paper are capable of much more advanced and complex techniques than what was possible in the past. Complex mathematical equations are often used to crease the paper in certain areas before folding to help create deeper dimensions, more realistic models, and more intricate folding sequences, which brings a whole new level of artistry into the wonderful art of origami.

The last significant difference is the purpose of origami. The tradition of using origami and origata for specific rituals still lives on, and while origami is still most commonly used as a fun pastime to make interesting decorations and gifts, this art has evolved into much more than that. With artists being given credit for their creations, great works of origami are appreciated for the artistic achievements they truly are and can be found in art exhibitions and galleries worldwide. New folding sequences are even created specifically for the purpose of constructing great works of art. The situations in which one gives origami as a gift have also changed significantly. Originally origami gifts were given on certain occasions, such as religious ceremonies, weddings, and funerals, where the gift has a specific cultural or spiritual meaning. While this custom still exists, origami gifts have become more common, and you can give a friend a cute little paper animal just because you feel like it. In modern times, the main purpose of giving an origami gift is to share your new art and show someone you care about them enough to put time and effort into making something for them, rather than just buying something. Origami has also become a nice way to present gifts, such as folding flowers to put on a card, boxes to put gifts in, or simple objects that reveal a loving message as you unfold them. It has also become popular to use origami with paper bills as a clever, creative way of gifting money to someone.

Pop culture and modern technology have also left their mark on modern origami. With computers and the internet, it's easier to get your hands on an origami sequence than ever, and even creating and sharing new diagrams is a breeze. This, together with the fact that it is an affordable art form, is one of the main reasons why origami is so incredibly popular today. Another reason why origami is so popular is the fact that it has been applied to all the best-loved movies, series, anime, and books. It will not be difficult to find instructions on how to fold your favorite movie character or icon out of paper.

Symbolism in Origami

In modern times, every single piece of origami and every fold doesn't hold a deeper meaning or symbolism as it once used to, but there are some old, traditional origami figures that still hold on to the cultural significance they once had during the Edo period. These are often given as a gift with a certain purpose and symbolism attached to them.

Boxes and Envelopes

Although decorative boxes and envelopes folded out of paper aren't strictly restricted to offerings and wedding gifts, it's still a popular custom to make your own boxes in which to present small gifts, as a way to show that you care and that the recipient is special to you. It is especially popular to give these handmade gifts to friends, family, and loved ones.

Samurai Helmets

Samurai are in Japanese culture what knights in shining armor are in ours. They are fierce, brave warriors who fight for the kingdom and slay evil beasts. The samurai have come to represent courage and chivalry, and of course manliness - every boy dreams of one day becoming a samurai at some point in his youth. An origami samurai helmet carries some of that symbolism and has become one of the most common icons of May 5th, which is a Japanese holiday called *Boy's Day* or *Children's Day*. This holiday celebrates the healthy birth and growth of children, especially boys. During this holiday, homes and buildings are often decorated with origami samurai helmets. Another popular custom on this day is to fold a large helmet using newspaper, which a child can wear all day long.

Tsuru

The crane is probably the most iconic origami figure in the world, even though it's a fairly complicated sequence. In Japanese culture, the crane is a majestic symbol of peace, fidelity, and longevity. This symbolism has in many ways been attached to the paper form of this bird. The crane is often folded and gifted as a prayer for peace, and because of its association with long life, it is also used to symbolize health and is often given to those who are ill or injured as a wish to get well soon.

The paper crane also has a very interesting legend surrounding it: it is believed that if one managed to fold 1,000 cranes, their single, deepest desire would be granted. Because of this belief and the association with health and long life, it has become a custom to make a *senbazuru*. A senbazuru is created by folding 1,000 cranes and tying them together with strings. These strings of cranes are then gifted to people who are severely ill or have suffered through a natural disaster. It's not unusual to see a senbazuru or two whenever you visit a hospital in Japan. The senbazuru has also come to represent a great wish for peace in the world.

Tatsu

Dragons have long been a symbol of power in Chinese, Japanese, and Vietnamese cultures, and although eastern dragons look quite different than the ones we know, there are origami sequences to fold both kinds. Origami dragons are usually folded to invite great fortune and success into your life, and they can also be created as a way to call for emotional strength during difficult times. Origami dragons are also given as gifts when someone is starting something new or taking an important step in life - like starting a new job, moving into a new home, or taking an important test or exam - and you want to wish them good luck.

Origami dragons can also be gifted or attached to a gift to wish someone success and good fortune in life in general.

Neko

Cats have always been an important part of Japanese culture and represent independence, wisdom, and mystery, and have long been a symbol of luck. It is believed that cats can bring great luck, especially when it comes to business, and to an extent, cats are associated with financial well-being. Cats are such an excellent good luck charm, that a cat figurine with a beckoning paw, also known as the *Maneki-Neko* has become a must-have for businesses all over Japan and China.

This beckoning cat can be found at the entrances of restaurants, shops, and even the offices of small businesses, all to welcome good luck and invite great business inside. Folding an origami cat and carrying it with you can be a great way to invite good luck and financial success into your life. There are dozens of folding sequences for origami cats, and you can even learn how to fold a Maneki-Neko specifically.

Kaeru

The Japanese word for 'frog' is also the Japanese word for 'return'. As such, the frog is a spiritual symbol of that which is lost being returned. Origami frogs are often folded and gifted in order to encourage this concept of having things returned to you. The most common custom is to carry a small origami frog in your wallet or purse, in the hopes that the money you are going to spend will be returned to you soon. As such, the frog represents sound investments and wisdom in financial matters. If you want the ultimate financial aid, you should always carry an origami cat and frog together, the cat inviting the fortune and wealth, and the frog ensuring that you work wisely when spending this wealth.

Another popular custom is to give origami frogs to people in order to ensure their return. When someone leaves on a journey, they are given a frog to wish them a safe journey and a safe return. If a child moves out of the house or a friend or family member moves far away, the frog they are given encourages them to visit soon and often.

Chocho

Butterflies have both positive and negative associations in different cultures, but in Japanese culture they have a very beautiful meaning. A butterfly represents all the hopes and wishes of a young girl as she transitions into womanhood. In Japanese culture, young girls often fold origami butterflies to somehow express and hold on to these hopes and dreams.

Two butterflies together carry a new meaning and represent a happy, blissful marriage. Because of this, paper butterflies are often used as decorations at weddings, and it is a popular custom to decorate any gifts presented to the bride and groom with a lovely pair of origami butterflies.

16

Symbols

Lines

———————————— Edge line. Shows the paper edge.

··· Creased line. Shows the fold line from the previous steps.

– – – – – – – Valley fold line. Shows the fold when paper edge is facing to the bottom.

—·—·—·—·—·— Mountain fold line. Shows the fold when paper edge is facing to the top.

··························· Imaginary line. Shows the paper position after the step is done.

Arrows

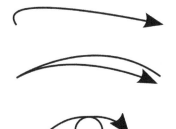

Direction arrow. Shows the direction to which paper will be folded.

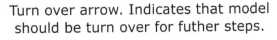

Fold and unfold arrow. Shows that only creased line needs to be done.

Turn over arrow. Indicates that model should be turn over for futher steps.

Squash arrow. Shows that paper has to be pushed down.

Rotation arrow. Shows the direction to which model should be rotated.

Folds

Valley Fold

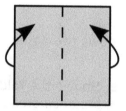 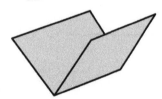

Folding the sides up while making the fold edge go down. Paper forms figure similar to the valley.

Mountain Fold

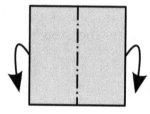 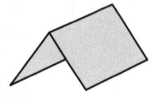

Folding the sides down while making the fold edge go up. Paper forms figure similar to the mountain.

Squash Fold

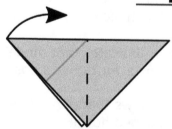 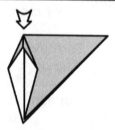 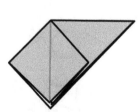

Fold containing two steps. First the corner is folded vertically up and then it is pushed down using already precreased lines.

Models List

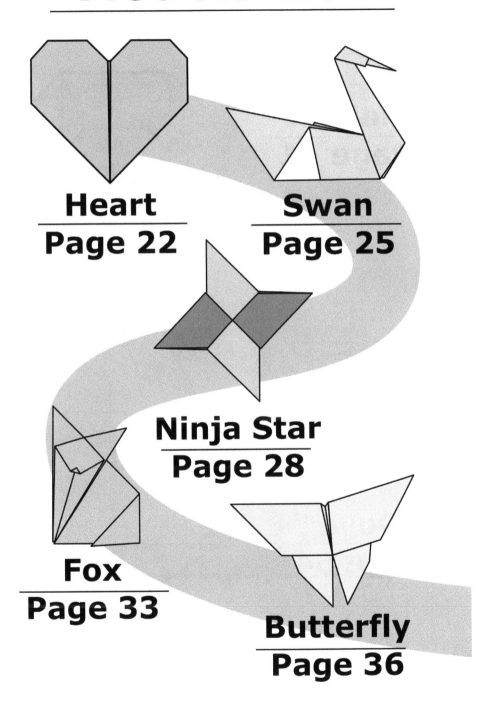

Heart

Swan

Ninja Star

Fox

Butterfly

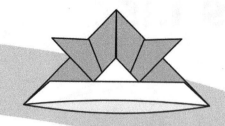

Helmet
Page 41

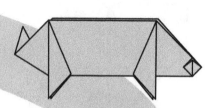

Pig
Page 45

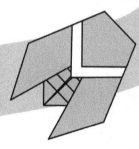

Cicada
Page 50

Dove
Page 54

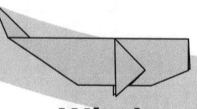

Whale
Page 58

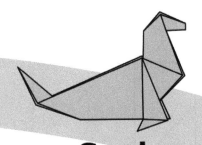

Seal
Page 62

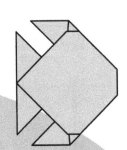

Fish
Page 67

Duck
Page 77

Rose
Page 72

Sailboat
Page 81

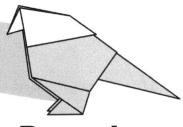

Parrot
Page 85

Heart

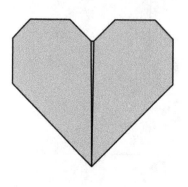

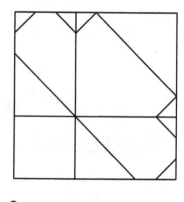

1 Start with the white side up.

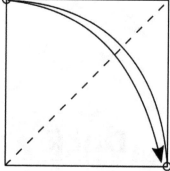

2 Fold and unfold in the half diagonally.

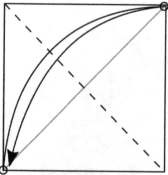

3 Fold and unfold in the half to the other direction.

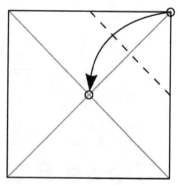

4 Fold the corner to the center point.

22

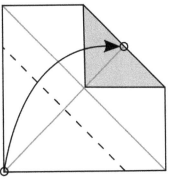

5 Fold the corner to the top middle point.

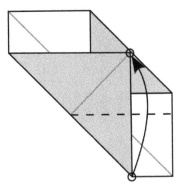

6 Fold the corner to the top middle point.

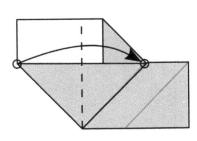

7 Fold the other corner accordingly.

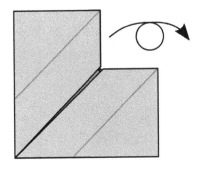

8 Turn the model over.

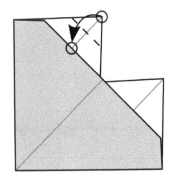

9 Fold the corner to the marked point.

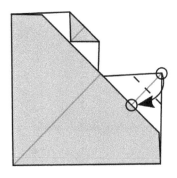

10 Fold the other corner accordingly.

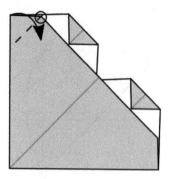

11 Fold corner according to the marked point.

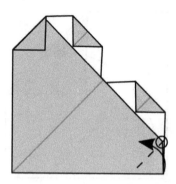

12 Fold the other corner accordingly.

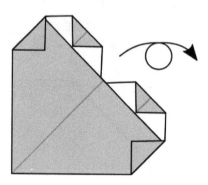

13 Turn the model over.

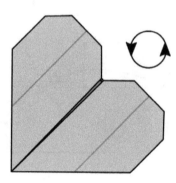

14 Rotate the model to the left.

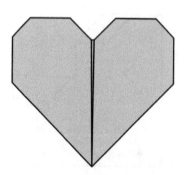

15 Finished heart!

Swan

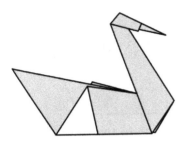

1 Start with the white side up.

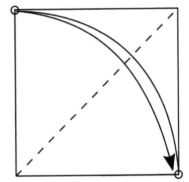

2 Fold and unfold in the half diagonally.

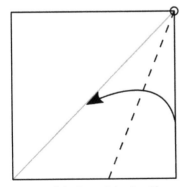

3 Fold the side to the diagonal line.

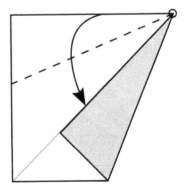

4 Fold the other side to the diagonal line.

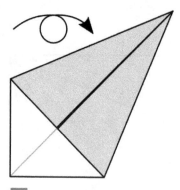

5 Turn the model over.

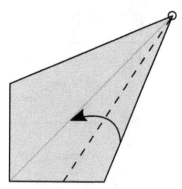

6 Fold the side to the digonal line.

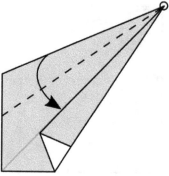

7 Fold the other side to the diagonal line.

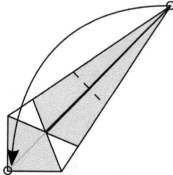

8 Fold the top corner to the bottom one.

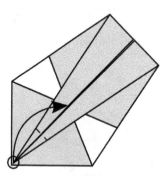

9 Fold the corner up.

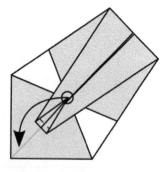

10 Fold the corner down.

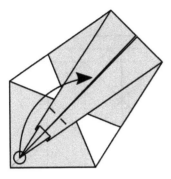

11 Fold the corner up to form the head.

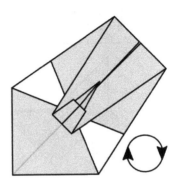

12 Rotate the model.

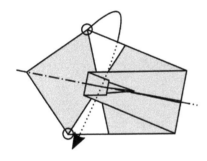

13 Fold the model in half behind.

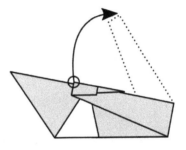

14 Lift the neck and head up.

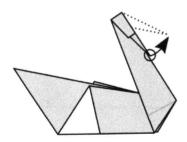

15 Lift the head up.

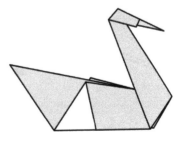

16 Finished swan!

Ninja Star

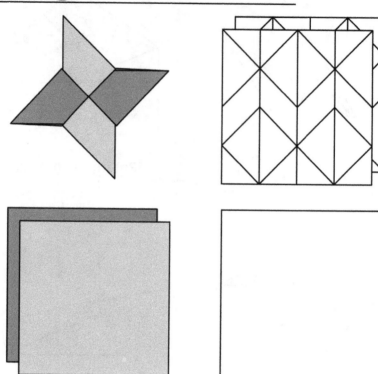

1 You will need two same size piece of papers.

2 Start with the white side up.

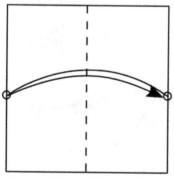

3 Fold and unfold vertically in the half.

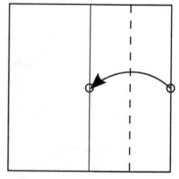

4 Fold the side to the center line.

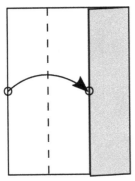

5 Fold the other side to the center line.

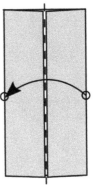

6 Fold the model in the half to the left.

7 Fold the corner diagonally down.

8 Fold the corner diagonally up.

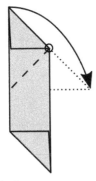

9 Fold the corner down as marked.

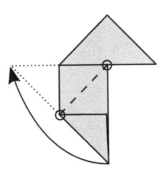

10 Fold the corner up as marked.

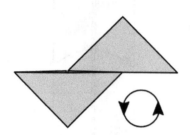

11 Rotate the model.

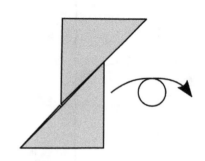

12 Turn the model over.

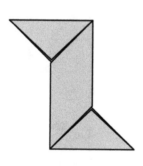

13 Finished first piece!

14 Start from step 7 with the other piece of paper.

15 Fold the corner diagonally down.

16 Fold the corner diagonally up.

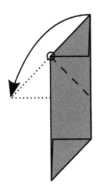

17 Fold the corner down as marked.

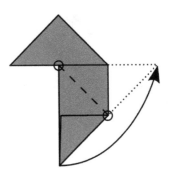

18 Fold the corner up as marked.

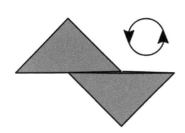

19 Rotate the model.

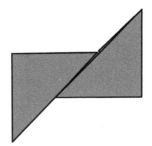

20 Finished second piece!

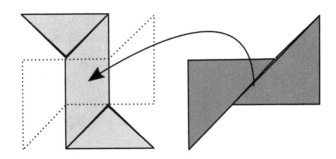

21 Put the second pieces on the top of the first one as indicated

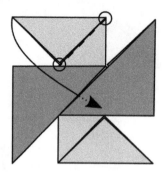

22 Tuck the corner inside the pocket.

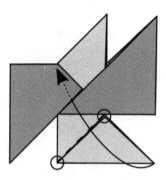

23 Tuck the other corner inside the pocket.

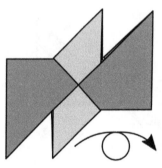

24 Turn the model over.

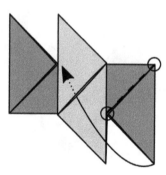

25 Tuck the corner inside the pocket.

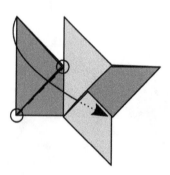

26 Tuck the last corner inside the pocket.

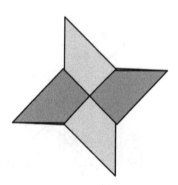

27 Finished ninja star!

Fox

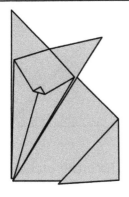

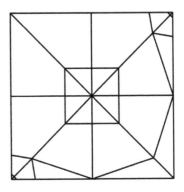

1 Start with the white side up.

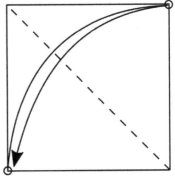

2 Fold and unfold in the half diagonally.

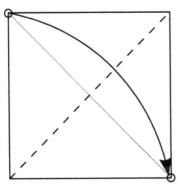

3 Fold diagonally in half to the other direction.

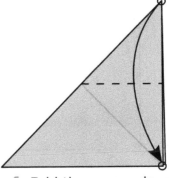

4 Fold the corner down to the bottom point.

33

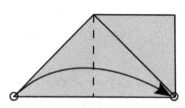

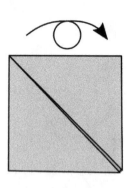

5 Fold the other corner to the same point.

6 Turn the model over.

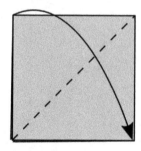

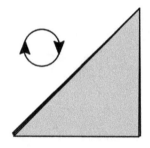

7 Fold the model diagonally in half.

8 Rotate the model.

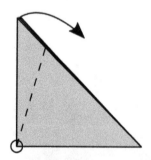

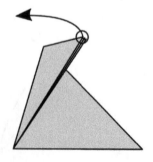

9 Fold through all the layers to the right.

10 Unfold the top layer back to the previous position.

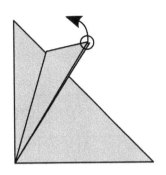

11 Fold the top layer perpendicularly up.

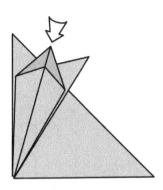

12 Squash fold down by separating layers to sides and pushing down the top part.

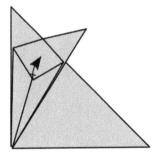

13 Fold the tip through the both layers up.

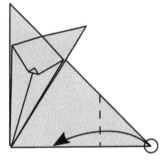

14 Fold the corner to the left.

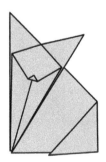

15 Finished fox!

Butterfly

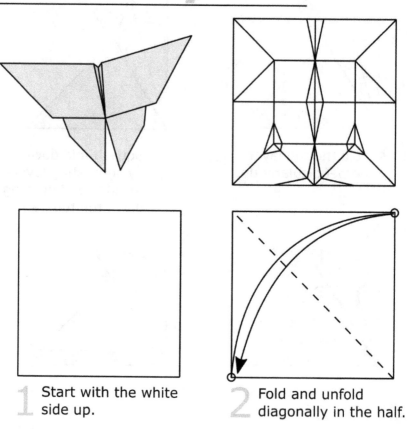

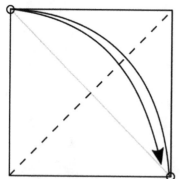

1 Start with the white side up.

2 Fold and unfold diagonally in the half.

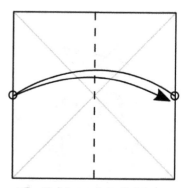

3 Fold and unfold diagonally in the half to the other direction.

4 Fold and unfold vertically in the half.

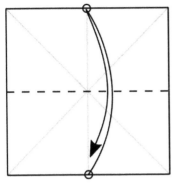

5 Fold and unfold horizontally in the half.

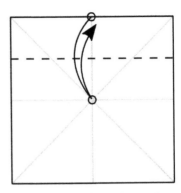

6 Fold and unfold the top edge to the center line.

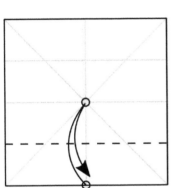

7 Fold and unfold the bottom edge to the center line.

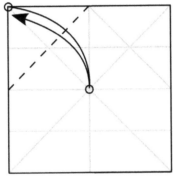

8 Fold and unfold the first corner to the center point.

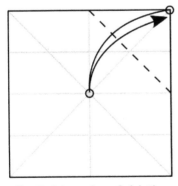

9 Fold and unfold the second corner to the center point.

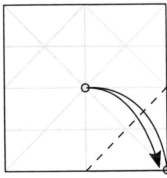

10 Fold and unfold the third corner to the center point.

37

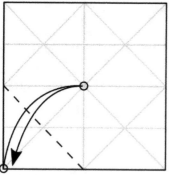

11 Fold and unfold the forth corner to the center point.

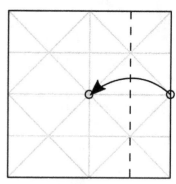

12 Fold the right edge to the center line.

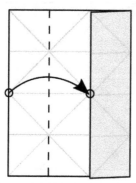

13 Fold the left edge to the center line.

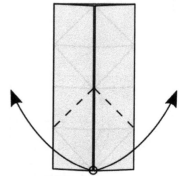

14 Fold the corners to the sides according to the marked lines.

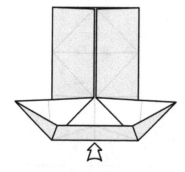

15 Squash the paper down to make it flat.

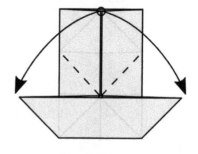

16 Fold the top corners to the sides.

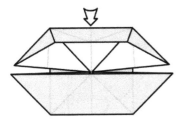

17 Squash the paper down to make it flat.

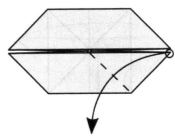

18 Fold the corner down.

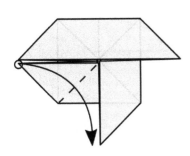

19 Fold the opposite corner down.

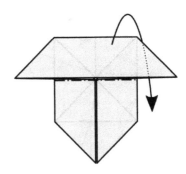

20 Fold the top part horizontally behind.

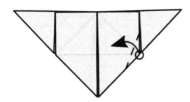

21 Fold the corner to the left.

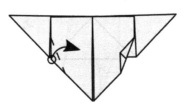

22 Fold the opposite corner to the right.

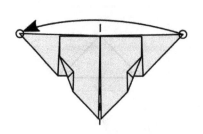

23 Fold the model in the hald to the left.

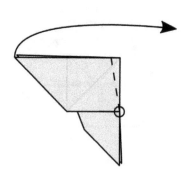

24 Fold the top layer to the right.

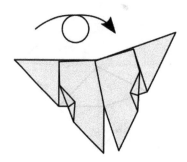

25 Turn the model over.

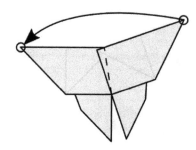

26 Fold the one corner to the other.

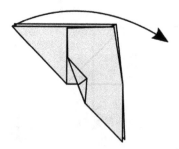

27 Open up the model by folding top layer to the right.

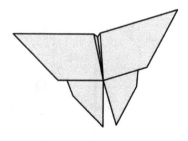

28 Finished butterfly!

Samurai Helmet

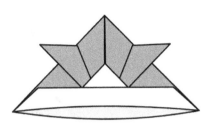

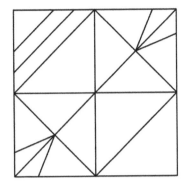

1 Start with the white side up.

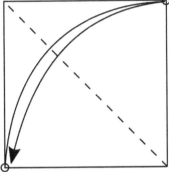

2 Fold and unfold in the half diagonally.

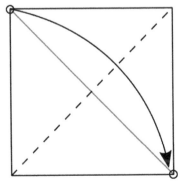

3 Fold diagonally in half to the other direction.

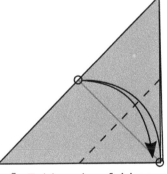

4 Fold and unfold corner to the top point.

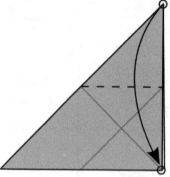

5 Fold the corner to the bottom point.

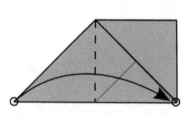

6 Fold the opposite corner to the bottom point.

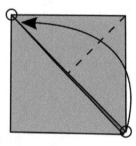

7 Fold the corner to the top point.

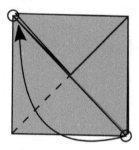

8 Fold the opposite corner to the top point.

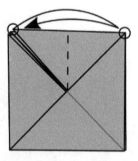

9 Fold and unfold the flap to the right corner.

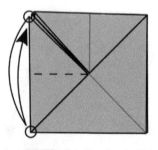

10 Fold and unfold the flap to the bottom corner.

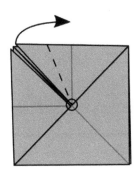

11 Fold the flap to the right on the line.

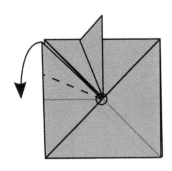

12 Fold the flap down on the line.

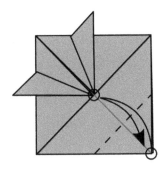

13 Fold and unfold the top layer to the top point.

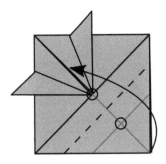

14 Fold the top layer up according to the marked points.

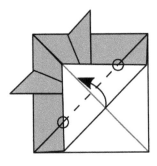

15 Fold the top layer up again according to the marked points.

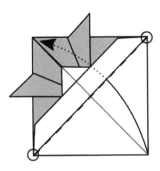

16 Fold the corner inside the model.

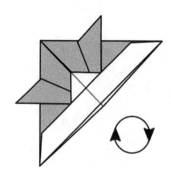

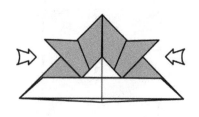

17 Fotate the model.

18 Push the sides to make the model 3D.

19 Finished samurai helmet!

Pig

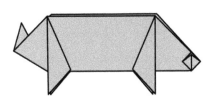

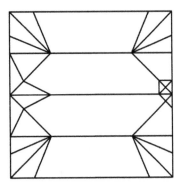

1 Start with the white side up.

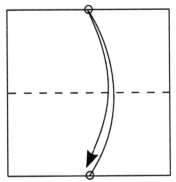

2 Fold and unfold horizontally in the half.

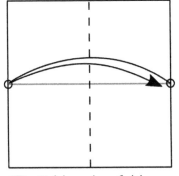

3 Fold and unfold vertically in the half.

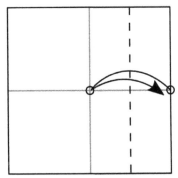

4 Fold and unfold the right side to the center line.

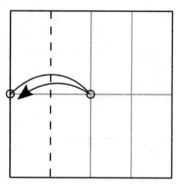

5 Fold and unfold the left side to the center line.

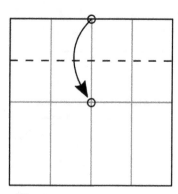

6 Fold the top edge to the center line.

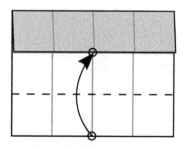

7 Fold the bottom edge to the center line.

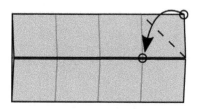

8 Fold the top right corner to the marked point.

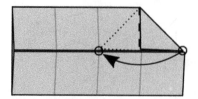

9 Take out the hidden corner to the left.

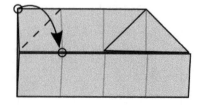

10 Fold the top left corner to the marked point.

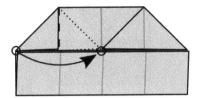

11 Take out the hidden corner to the right.

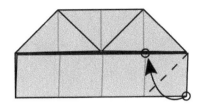

12 Fold the bottom right corner to the marked point.

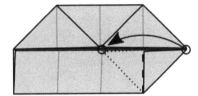

13 Take out the hidden corner ro the left.

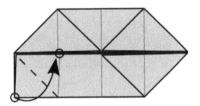

14 Fold the bottom left corner to the marked point.

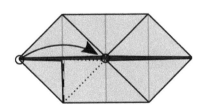

15 Take out the hidden corner to the right.

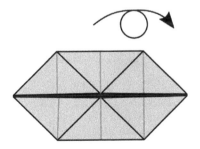

16 Turn the model over.

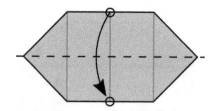

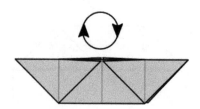

17 Fold the model horizontally in the half.

18 Rotate the model.

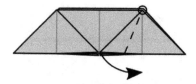

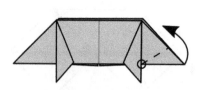

19 Fold the corner down to the right.

20 Fold the corner down to the left.

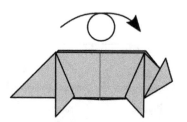

21 Fold the corner up.

22 Turn the model over.

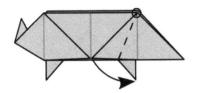

23 Fold the corner down to the right.

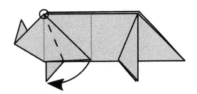

24 Fold the corner down to the left.

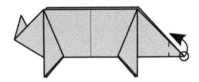

25 Fold the corner perpendicurlarly up.

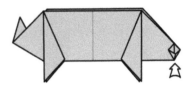

26 Squash fold the corner down by separating layers to the sides.

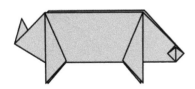

27 Finished pig!

Cicada

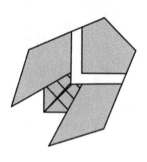

1 Start with the white side up.

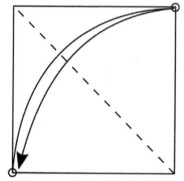

2 Fold and unfold in the half diagonally.

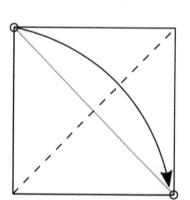

3 Fold diagonally in half to the other direction.

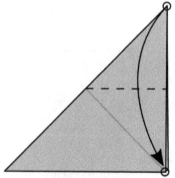

4 Fold the corner down to the bottom point.

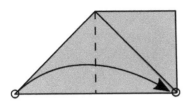 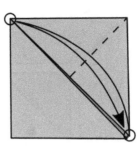

5 Fold the corner to the same point.

6 Fold and unfold the corner to the top point.

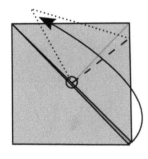 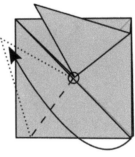

7 Fold the corner up according to the marked point.

8 Fold the other corner up according to the marked point.

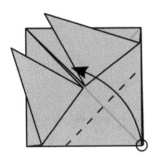 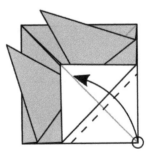

9 Fold the top layer up on the center line.

10 Fold the bottom layer up on the center line.

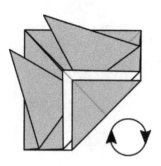

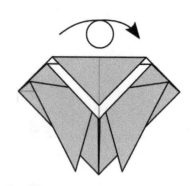

11 Rotate the model.

12 Turn the model over.

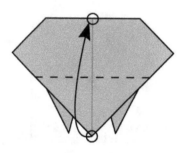

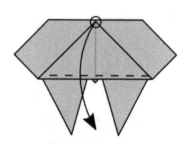

13 Fold the corner to the top middle point.

14 Fold the corner down leaving a little space between the folds.

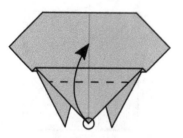

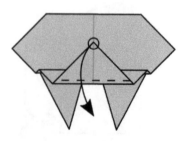

15 Fold the corner up on the middle line.

16 Fold the corner down leaving a little space between the folds.

52

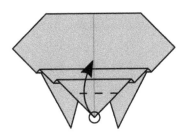

17 Fold the corner up on the middle line.

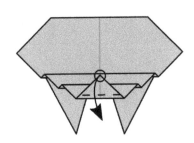

18 Fold the corner down leaving a little space between the folds.

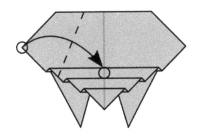

19 Fold the left edge on the center line.

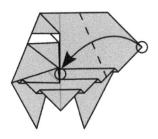

20 Fold the right edge on the center line.

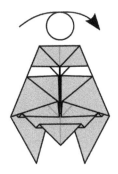

21 Turn the model over.

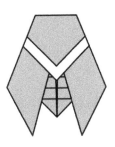

22 Finished cicada!

Dove

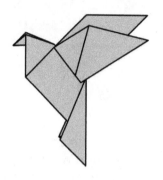

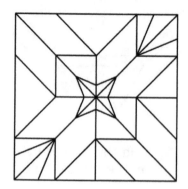

1 Start with the white side up.

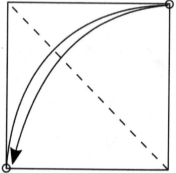

2 Fold and unfold in the half diagonally.

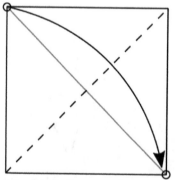

3 Fold diagonally in half to the other direction.

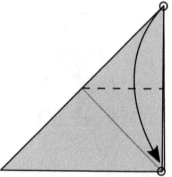

4 Fold the corner down to the bottom point.

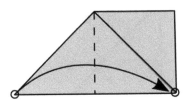

5 Fold the other corner to the same point.

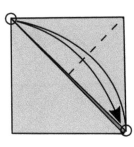

6 Fold and unfold the corner to the top point.

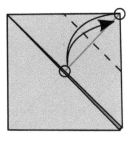

7 Fold and unfold the top right corner to the marked point.

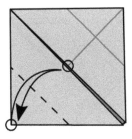

8 Fold and unfold the bottom left corner to the marked point.

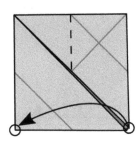

9 Fold the bottom right corner to the bottom left corner.

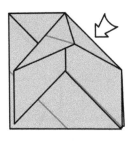

10 Squash the paper down to make the model lie flat.

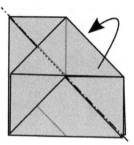

11 Fold the model in the half by folding right part behind.

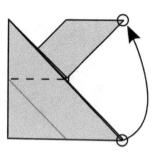

12 Fold the bottom right corner to the top right corner.

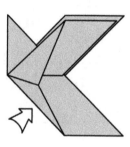

13 Squash the paper down to make the model lie flat.

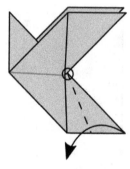

14 Fold the corner down according to the marked point.

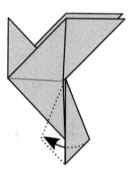

15 Take out the hidden paper layer to the left.

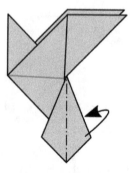

16 Fold the right edge behind.

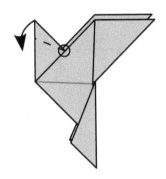

17 Fold the corner down according to the marked point.

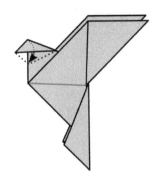

18 Take out the hidden paper layer down.

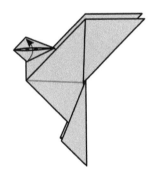

19 Fold the bottom edge to the top.

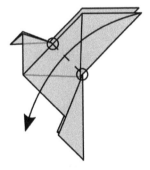

20 Fold the corner down according to the marked points.

21 Fold the corner back up according to the marked point.

22 Finished dove!

Whale

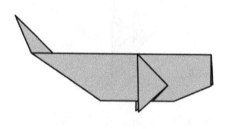

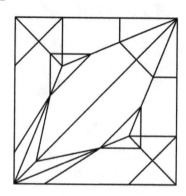

1 Start with the white side up.

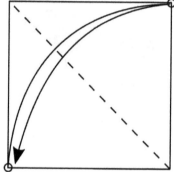

2 Fold and unfold in the half diagonally.

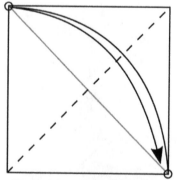

3 Fold and unfold diagonally in the half to the other direction.

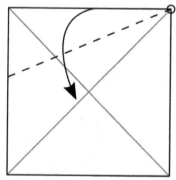

4 Fold the top edge to the center line.

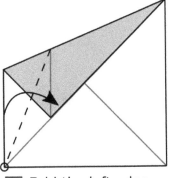

5 Fold the left edge to the center line.

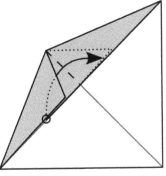

6 Take out the hidden corner to the top.

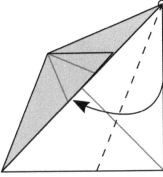

7 Fold the right edge to the center line.

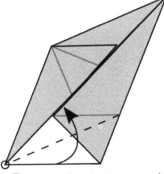

8 Fold the bottom edge to the center line.

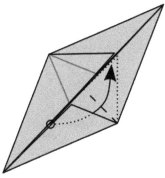

9 Take out the hidden corner to the top.

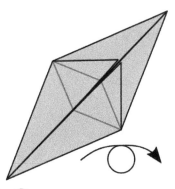

10 Turn the model over.

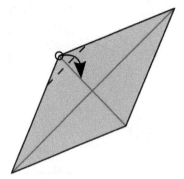

11 Fold the corner on the center line.

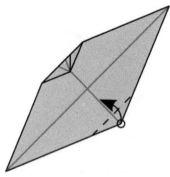

12 Fold the opposite corner on the center line.

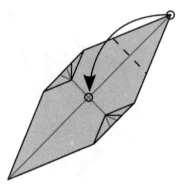

13 Fold the top corner to the center point.

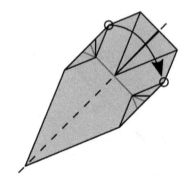

14 Fold the model in the half.

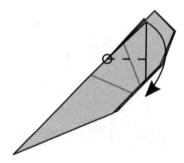

15 Fold the corner down accroding to the marked point.

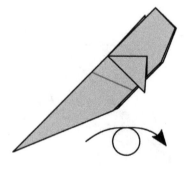

16 Turn the model over.

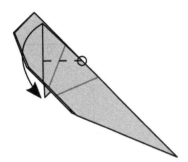

17 Fold the corner down according to the marked point.

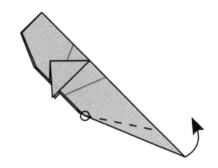

18 Fold the corner up according to the marked point.

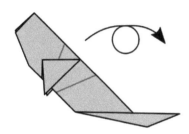

19 Turn the model over.

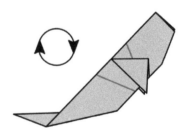

20 Rotate the model.

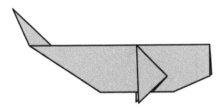

21 Finished whale!

Seal

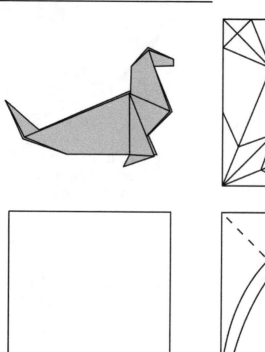

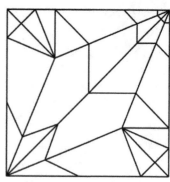

1 Start with the white side up.

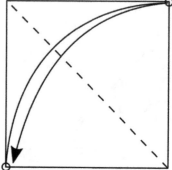

2 Fold and unfold in the half diagonally.

3 Fold and unfold diagonally in the half to the other direction.

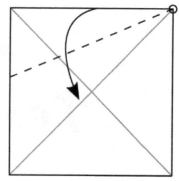

4 Fold the top edge to the center line.

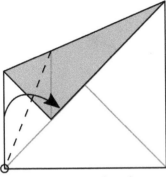

5 Fold the left edge to the center line.

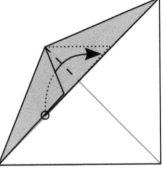

6 Take out the hidden corner to the top.

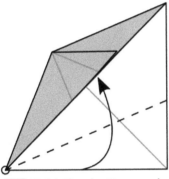

7 Fold the bottom edge to the center line.

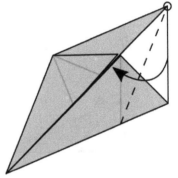

8 Fold the right edge to the center line.

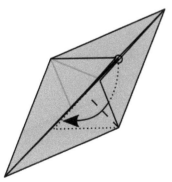

9 Take out the hidden corner to the bottom.

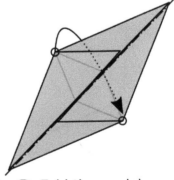

10 Fold the model behind in the half.

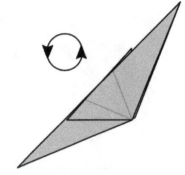

11 Rotate the model.

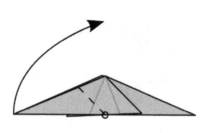

12 Fold the corner up according to the market point.

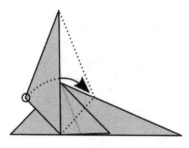

13 Take out the hidden corner to the right.

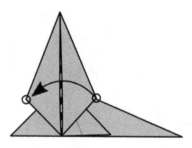

14 Fold the corner to the left.

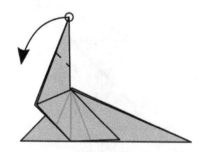

15 Fold the corner vertically down.

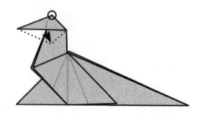

16 Take out the hidden corner down.

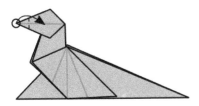

17 Fold the corner on the middle line.

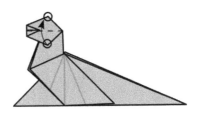

18 Fold the corner to the top point.

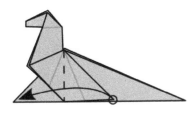

19 Fold the corner to the left.

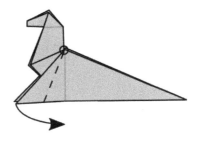

20 Fold the corner down according to the marked point.

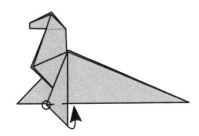

21 Fold the corner vertically up.

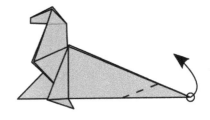

22 Fold the corner up.

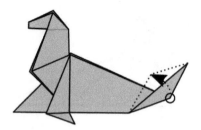

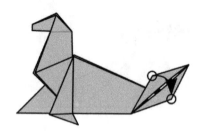

23 Take out the hidden corner to the left.

24 Fold the corner to the left.

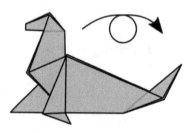

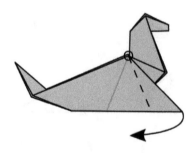

25 Turn over the model.

26 Fold the corner down according to the marked point.

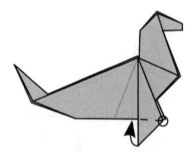

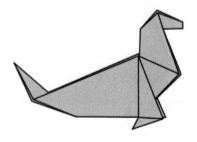

27 Fold the coroner vertically up.

28 Finished seal!

Fish

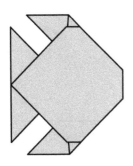

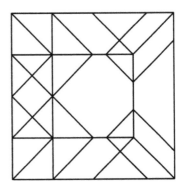

1 Start with the white side up.

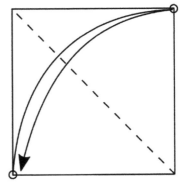

2 Fold and unfold diagonally in the half.

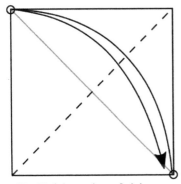

3 Fold and unfold diagonally in the half to the other direction.

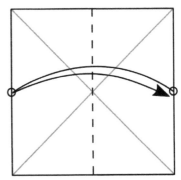

4 Fold and unfold vertically in the half.

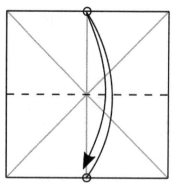

5 Fold and unfold horizontally in the half.

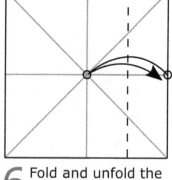

6 Fold and unfold the right edge to the center line.

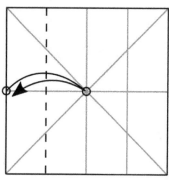

7 Fold and unfold the left edge to the center line.

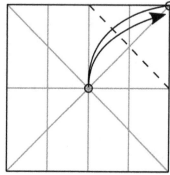

8 Fold and unfold the top right corner to the center point.

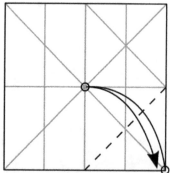

9 Fold and unfold the bottom right corner to the center point.

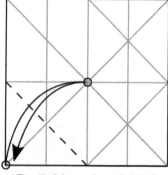

10 Fold and unfold the bottom left corner to the center point.

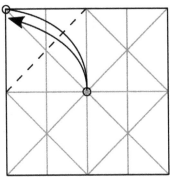

11 Fold and unfold the top left corner to the center point.

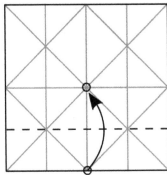

12 Fold the bottom edge to the center line.

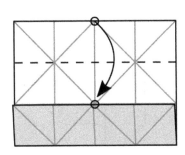

13 Fold the top edge to the center line.

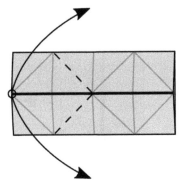

14 Fold the corners to the sides according to the marked lines.

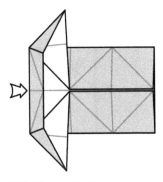

15 Squash the paper down to make it flat.

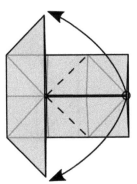

16 Fold the corner to the sides according to the marked lines.

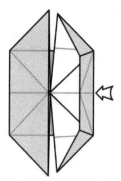

17 Squash the paper down to make it flat.

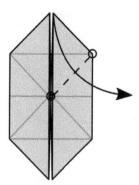

18 Fold the corner down according to the marked point.

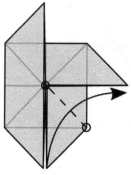

19 Fold the corner up according to the marked points.

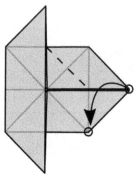

20 Fold the corner to the bottom point.

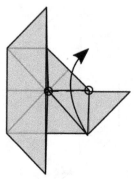

21 Fold the corner up according to the marked points.

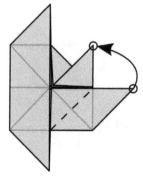

22 Fold the corner to the top point.

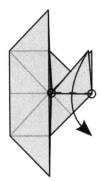

23 Fold the corner down accroding to the marked points.

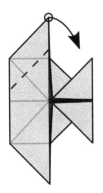

24 Fold the corner diagonally down.

25 Fold the corner diagonally up.

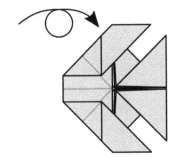

26 Turn the model over.

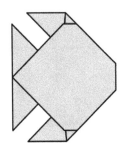

27 Finished fish!

Rose

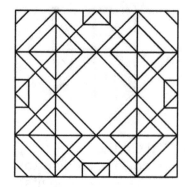

1 Start with the white side up.

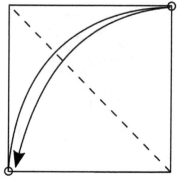

2 Fold and unfold in the half diagonally.

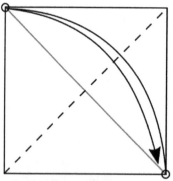

3 Fold and unfold diagonally in the half to the other direction.

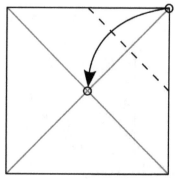

4 Fold the top right corner to the center point.

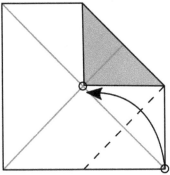

5 Fold the bottom right corner to the center point.

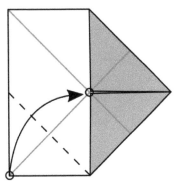

6 Fold the bottom left corner to the center point.

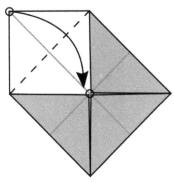

7 Fold the top left corner to the center point.

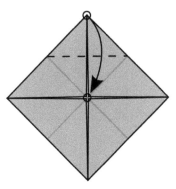

8 Fold the top corner to the center point.

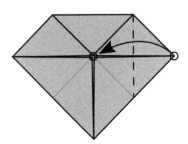

9 Fold the right corner to the center point.

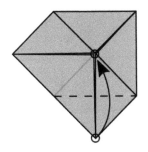

10 Fold the bottom corner to the center point.

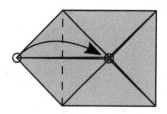

11 Fold the left corner to the center point.

12 Fold the top right corner to the center point.

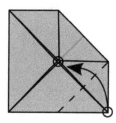

13 Fold the bottom right corner to the center point.

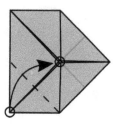

14 Fold the bottom left corner to the center point.

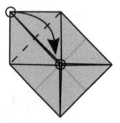

15 Fold the top left corner to the center point.

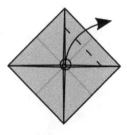

16 Fold the corner outside to the top right.

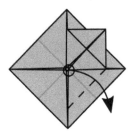

17 Fold the corner outside to the bottom right.

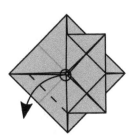

18 Fold the corner outside to the bottom left.

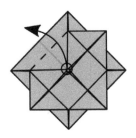

19 Fold the corner outside to the top left.

20 Fold the corner from the center to the top.

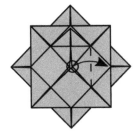

21 Fold the corner from the center to the right.

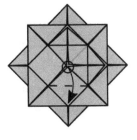

22 Fold the corner from the center to the bottom.

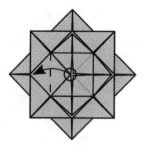

23 Fold the corner from the center to the left.

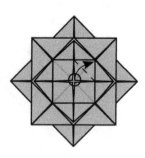

24 Fold the corner to the top right.

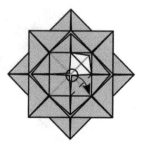

25 Fold the corner to the bottom right.

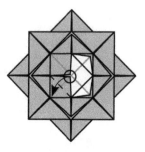

26 Fold the corner to the bottom left.

27 Fold the corner to the top left.

28 Finished rose!

Duck

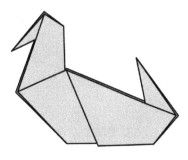

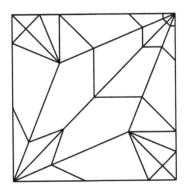

1 Start with the white side up.

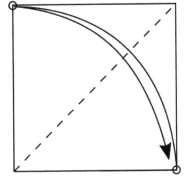

2 Fold and unfold in the half diagonally.

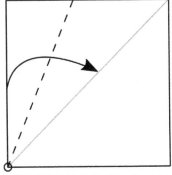

3 Fold the left edge to the center line.

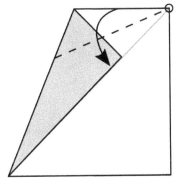

4 Fold the top edge to the center line.

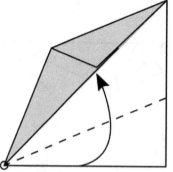

5 Fold the bottom edge to the center line.

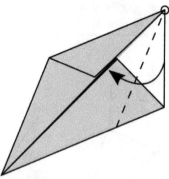

6 Fold the right edge to the center line.

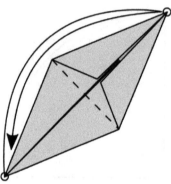

7 Fold and unfold diagonally in the half.

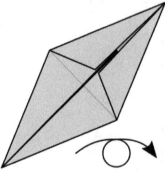

8 Turn the model over.

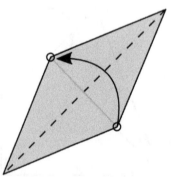

9 Fold the model in half to the top point.

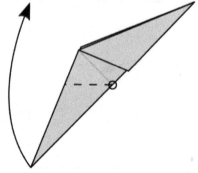

10 Fold the corner up accordin to the marked point.

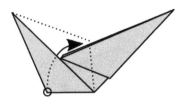

11 Take out the hidden corner to the right.

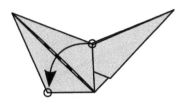

12 Fold the corner to the left.

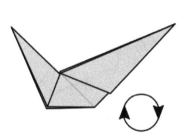

13 Rotate the model.

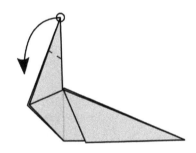

14 Fold the corner down.

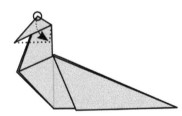

15 Take out the hidden corner down.

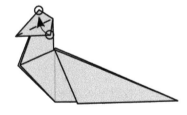

16 Fold the corner up.

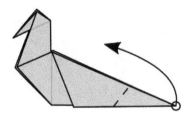

17 Fold the corner up.

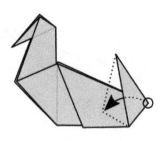

18 Take out the hidden corner to the left.

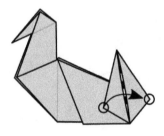

19 Fold the corner to the right.

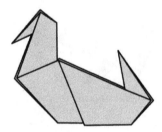

20 Finished duck!

Sailboat

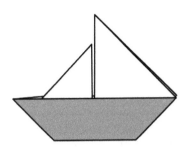

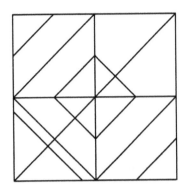

1 Start with the white side up.

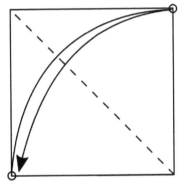

2 Fold and unfold in the half diagonally.

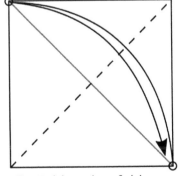

3 Fold and unfold diagonally in the half to the other direction.

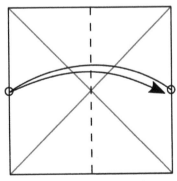

4 Fold and unfold vertically in the half.

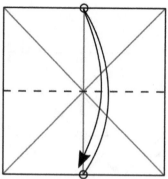

5 Fold and unfold horizontally in the half.

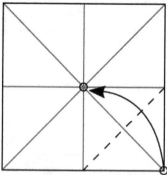

6 Fold the bottom right corner to the center point.

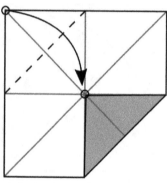

7 Fold the top left corner to the center point.

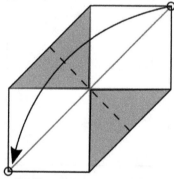

8 Fold the top right corner to the bottom left corner.

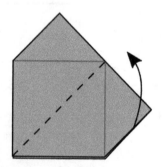

9 Fold the left edge vertically up.

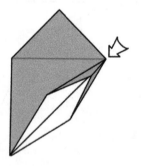

10 Squash fold the edge down to make the model flat.

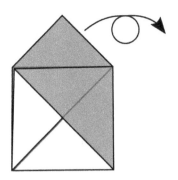

11 Turn the model over.

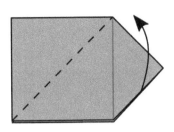

12 Fold the left edge vertically up.

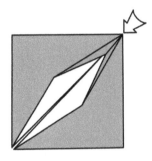

13 Squash fold the edge down to make the model flat.

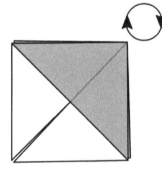

14 Rotate the model.

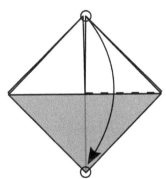

15 Fold the top left corner to the bottom point.

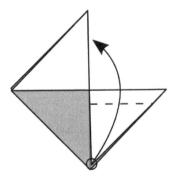

16 Fold the corner up.

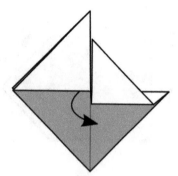

17 Bring the paper layer from behind to the front.

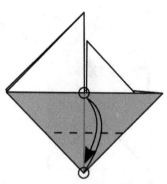

18 Fold and unfold the bottom corner to the center point.

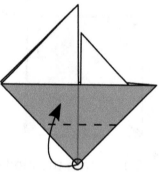

19 Fold the bottom corner vertically up.

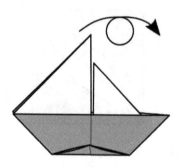

20 Turn the model over.

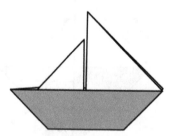

21 Finished sailboat!

Parrot

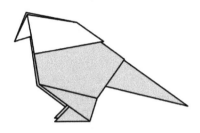

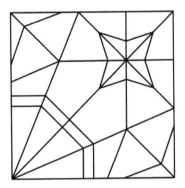

1 Start with the white side up.

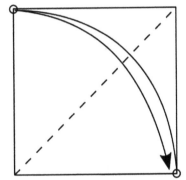

2 Fold and unfold in the half diagonally.

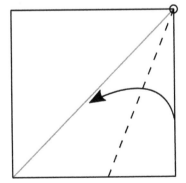

3 Fold the left edge to the center line.

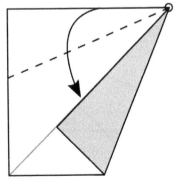

4 Fold the top edge to the center line.

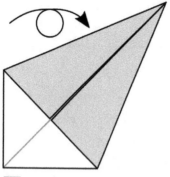

5 Turn the model over.

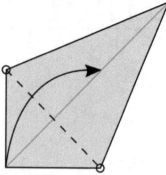

6 Fold the corner up according to the marked points.

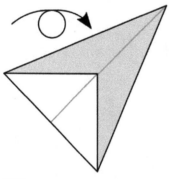

7 Turn the model over.

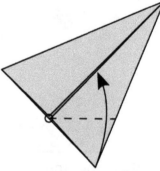

8 Fold the corner to the center line according to the marked point.

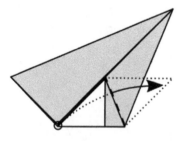

9 Take out the hidden corner to the right.

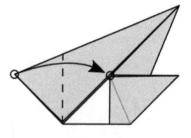

10 Fold the corner to the marked point.

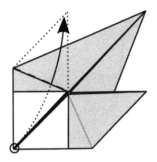

11 Take out the hidden corner to the top.

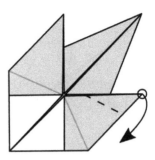

12 Fold the corner down.

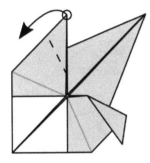

13 Fold the opposite corner symmetrically down.

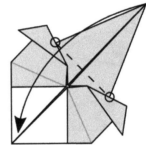

14 Fold the corner down according to the marked points.

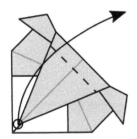

15 Fold the corner up.

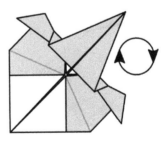

16 Rotate the model.

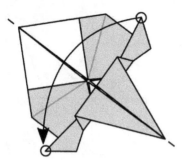

17 Fold the model in down in half.

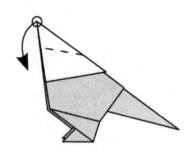

18 Fold the corner down.

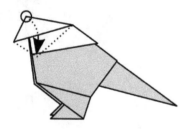

19 Take out the hidden corner to the bottom.

20 Fold the corner to the top point.

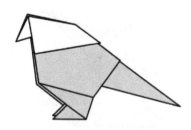

21 Finished parrot!

PS: Can I Ask You for a Quick Favor?

First of all, thank you for purchasing **Origami Book for Beginners!** I know that you could have picked any number of books to read, but you picked this one and for that I am extremely grateful.

If you enjoyed this book and found some benefit in reading it, I'd like to hear from you and hope that you could take some time to post a review if possible.

Your feedback and support will help me to greatly improve my writing craft for future projects and make this book even better.

THANKS!

=)

Printed in the USA
CPSIA information can be obtained
at www.ICGtesting.com
LVHW010545261123
764840LV00004B/627